My Teacher Well-Being Journal

My Teacher Well-Being Journal
Copyright © Chris Allton, 2021
First published by Chris Allton 2021 via Amazon Kindle Direct Publishing
www.chrisallton.co.uk
ISBN - 9798678753458
Front cover design © 2021 by Chris Allton

My Teacher Well-Being Journal

This journal is not designed to be a diary you use at school. You know, the one with bits of paper and lots of crossings out. That diary may often cause stress every time you look at it. This journal is designed to improve your well-being, and we all need a bit of well-being, don't we. So, what does this journal offer.

Well, it is about you. It is looking at your goals, both academic and personal. For you to create some positive affirmations about yourself and your day. Think of your goals and those around you; how you will make the coming week great and reflect on all that is good and plan for the following week. Not lessons but plan your own wellbeing. You may find you will not even take this journal into school but fill it in in a morning, after school or before bedtime. It is to remind you that you are a good teacher and all the good things that happen to you in your life.

Weeks start on a Sunday so that when you look at a new week it starts with something great you have done over the weekend, not a lesson observation or OFSTED. This is a positive journal for your positive thoughts. Your job is hard enough without worrying about your own negative thoughts. The weekly plans continue throughout holidays and the summer break because your mindfulness does not stop then. That is when you recharge and reflect on the half term.

Fill in the year planner at the start with holidays, weekend plans and ways of self-improvement. Spread the love with work colleagues and share your positive affirmations. Look at your mood tracker each week and see what areas of your life you need to prioritise further. Set goals and rewards for yourself and share the positive quotes used throughout. Doodle in the margins and do mindful colouring. There are hidden tips and hints to help you relax and reflect and be the great teacher that you are.

Name: . . . .

School: . . . .

Roles: . . . .

Roles at Home: . . . .

. . . .

Values: . . . .

. . . .

Strengths: . . . .

. . . .

Mission Statement: . . . .

. . . .

. . . .

. . . .

. . . .

. . . .

. . . .

. . . .

September	October	November
1	1	1
2	2	2
3	3	3
4	4	4
5	5	5
6	6	6
7	7	7
8	8	8
9	9	9
10	10	10
11	11	11
12	12	12
13	13	13
14	14	14
15	15	15
16	16	16
17	17	17
18	18	18
19	19	19
20	20	20
21	21	21
22	22	22
23	23	23
24	24	24
25	25	25
26	26	26
27	27	27
28	28	28
29	29	29
30	30	30
	31	
Highlight your holidays – the time to recharge		

December	January	February
1	1	1
2	2	2
3	3	3
4	4	4
5	5	5
6	6	6
7	7	7
8	8	8
9	9	9
10	10	10
11	11	11
12	12	12
13	13	13
14	14	14
15	15	15
16	16	16
17	17	17
18	18	18
19	19	19
20	20	20
21	21	21
22	22	22
23	23	23
24	24	24
25	25	25
26	26	26
27	27	27
28	28	28
29	29	
30	30	
31	31	
Highlight you weekends – things to look forward to		

March	April	May
1	1	1
2	2	2
3	3	3
4	4	4
5	5	5
6	6	6
7	7	7
8	8	8
9	9	9
10	10	10
11	11	11
12	12	12
13	13	13
14	14	14
15	15	15
16	16	16
17	17	17
18	18	18
19	19	19
20	20	20
21	21	21
22	22	22
23	23	23
24	24	24
25	25	25
26	26	26
27	27	27
28	28	28
29	29	29
30	30	30
31		31
Highlight your training – self improvement		

June	July	August
1	1	1
2	2	2
3	3	3
4	4	4
5	5	5
6	6	6
7	7	7
8	8	8
9	9	9
10	10	10
11	11	11
12	12	12
13	13	13
14	14	14
15	15	15
16	16	16
17	17	17
18	18	18
19	19	19
20	20	20
21	21	21
22	22	22
23	23	23
24	24	24
25	25	25
26	26	26
27	27	27
28	28	28
29	29	29
30	30	30
	31	31

Highlight assessments – track your improvements

Goals for The Year:

1.

2.

3.

4.

5.

6.

To Do This Year

1.

2.

3.

4.

5.

6.

Headteacher Expectations This Year

1.

2.

3.

4.

5.

6.

Expectations of Myself

1.

2.

3.

4.

5.

6.

Expectations of My Teaching Assistant

1.

2.

3.

4.

5.

6.

Expectations of My Pupils

1.

2.

3.

4.

5.

6.

Amusing/ Kind Things Said by Other Staff/ Parents/ Children

Positive Affirmations

Here are some examples of positive affirmations you may use in your weekly plan. The first five weeks have examples in.

- I am calm.
- I will not worry about things out of my control.
- I have nothing to worry about.
- I am free from constraints.
- I choose to exist right now.
- I am here in the present moment.
- I have the power to change what does not serve me.
- I will focus on what makes me happy.
- Challenges only bring me closer to my goals.
- I will be mindful and aware of my body and space.
- I attract positive energy.
- I am prioritizing my happiness.
- My mind is calm.
- I am free to let go of fear.
- I will not be held back by the past.
- I create the world I am in.
- I surrender my fear and doubts, as they do not serve me.
- All is well in this moment.
- My thoughts are not me.
- I choose to replace worry with love and acceptance
- Today I love my body fully, deeply and joyfully.
- I choose to see the divine perfection in every cell of my body.
- I love myself and I allow others to love me too.

- My well-being is my top priority.
- I know that I can master anything if I do it enough times.
- I am open to abundance in all aspects of life.
- My grateful heart is a magnet that attracts everything I desire.
- My unique skills and talents can make a profound difference in the world.
- I am meant to do great things.
- I am limited only by my vision of what is possible.
- What I experience today will lead me to greatness.
- Today I release fear and open my heart to true love.
- My inner voice guides me in the right direction.
- I am centred, calm and mindful.
- I do not have to be perfect; I just have to be me.
- I am my best cheerleader.
- I am unique for my qualities and talents.
- I am proud of myself for even daring to try; many people will not even do that!
- I let go of hesitations and welcome in prosperity.
- All is well, right here, right now.
- I seize every opportunity.
- An opportunity is simply a possibility until I act on it.
- I am grateful for the people in my life.
- I love myself radically.
- My body is a projection of my soul and beliefs.
- Fear is only a feeling; it cannot hold me back.
- I have everything I need to prosper.
- As my commitment to help others grows, so does my wealth.

Week commencing – Example week
This week - I am showing gratitude for: 1. *Fellow staff supporting me* 2. *The sun shining when I wake up* 3. *A fabulous summer holiday*
I will make this week great by: 1. *Smiling to staff* 2. *Asking each child about their holiday* 3. *Performing an act of random kindness*
This week's goals: 1. *Welcome children back into school* 2. *Update co-ordinators file* 3. *Assess reading ages of children*
Rewards if achieved: 1. *Bottle of wine on Friday* 2. *Shopping trip on Saturday* 3. *Family walk on Sunday*
Positive affirmations: 1. *I am grateful for the people in my life.* 2. *I am open to abundance in all aspects of life.* 3. *I will focus on what makes me happy.*
Quote: *"Education is the most powerful weapon which you can use to change the world"* – Nelson Mandela.

Sunday
Family dinner to celebrate birthday followed by a lovely walk.

Monday
INSET – phonics update and time to develop a positive learning environment

Tuesday
Staff meeting at 12.30

Wednesday
Discuss after school clubs

Thursday
Staff meeting after school – Literacy planning

Friday
Zoom assembly at 9am. *Dinner time club.*

Saturday
Shopping trip

Week Reflection

What have I learnt this week?
Started a coding course with the children so we learn together.

What am I grateful for?
The help from fellow staff members

What emotions have I felt?
Worry, joy, exhaustion

What distractions or fears have I encountered and how did I meet them?
Worry – asked for help
Exhaustion – gave time for me

Habit Tracker (out of 10)

Habit	M	T	W	T	F	S	S
Mood	9	9	8	7	8	10	10
Purpose	9	8	8	8	9	7	5
You Time	5	5	5	5	6	8	9
Healthy Eating	7	7	6	5	7	8	7
Drinking Water	9	9	9	8	9	6	5
Exercise	4	8	5	4	7	9	5
Children time	4	5	5	5	5	8	10
Partner time	4	4	5	5	5	7	10
Gym time	0	0	8	0	0	8	0

What have I rewarded myself with this week and what was it for?

I achieved all the goals set so I had that bottle of wine on Friday evening. On Saturday I enjoyed a shopping trip and got some nice things for the house as a reward. On Sunday we all went out for a walk in the country and even though it rained we all laughed a lot and I feel so grateful for what I have.

How can I make next week even better and what do I need to prepare?

I will do another act of random kindness next week. I need to plan observations for PE and Maths and speak to the head about my development plan and its funding. I am feeling positive about the new week and confident in my proposal for the headteacher.

I need to assess the children's Maths level and adapt planning accordingly.

Week commencing – 29 August
This week -   I am showing gratitude for: 1.   2.   3.
I will make this week great by: 1.   2.   3.
This week's goals: 1.   2.   3.
Rewards if achieved: 1.   2.   3.
Positive affirmations: 1. *I will not worry about things out of my control.*   2.   3.
Quote: *"Live as if you were to die tomorrow. Learn as if you were to live forever"* – Mahatma Gandhi

Sunday – *Find three things to look forward to this week*
Monday
Tuesday
Wednesday
Thursday
Friday
Saturday

Week Reflection

What have I learnt this week?

What am I grateful for?

What emotions have I felt?

What distractions or fears have I encountered and how did I meet them?

Habit Tracker (out of 10)

Habit	M	T	W	T	F	S	S
Mood							
Purpose							
You Time							
Healthy Eating							
Drinking Water							
Exercise							

What have I rewarded myself with this week and what was it for?

How can I make next week even better and what do I need to prepare?

Week commencing – 5 September
This week - I am showing gratitude for: 1. 2. 3.
I will make this week great by: 1. 2. 3.
This week's goals: 1. 2. 3.
Rewards if achieved: 1. 2. 3.
Positive affirmations: 1. *I have nothing to worry about.* 2. 3.
Quote: *"The cure for boredom is curiosity. There is no cure for curiosity"* – Dorothy Parker

Sunday
Monday – *Make time to do something kind for yourself*
Tuesday
Wednesday
Thursday
Friday
Saturday

Week Reflection

What have I learnt this week?

What am I grateful for?

What emotions have I felt?

What distractions or fears have I encountered and how did I meet them?

Habit Tracker (out of 10)

Habit	M	T	W	T	F	S	S
Mood							
Purpose							
You Time							
Healthy Eating							
Drinking Water							
Exercise							

What have I rewarded myself with this week and what was it for?

How can I make next week even better and what do I need to prepare?

Week commencing – 12 September
This week -   I am showing gratitude for: 1.   2.   3.
I will make this week great by: 1.   2.   3.
This week's goals: 1.   2.   3.
Rewards if achieved: 1.   2.   3.
Positive affirmations: 1. *I am free from constraints.*   2.   3.
Quote: *"If You are planning for a year, sow rice; if you are planning for a decade, plant trees; if you are planning for a lifetime, educate people"* – Chinese Proverb

Sunday

Monday

Tuesday – *Do something kind for someone else*

Wednesday

Thursday

Friday

Saturday

Week Reflection

What have I learnt this week?

What am I grateful for?

What emotions have I felt?

What distractions or fears have I encountered and how did I meet them?

Habit Tracker (out of 10)

Habit	M	T	W	T	F	S	S
Mood							
Purpose							
You Time							
Healthy Eating							
Drinking Water							
Exercise							

What have I rewarded myself with this week and what was it for?

How can I make next week even better and what do I need to prepare?

Week commencing – 19 September

This week -
I am showing gratitude for:
1.
2.
3.

I will make this week great by:
1.
2.
3.

This week's goals:
1.
2.
3.

Rewards if achieved:
1.
2.
3.

Positive affirmations:
1. *I choose to exist right now.*
2.
3.

Quote: *"It's not that I'm so smart, it's just that I stay with problems longer"* – Albert Einstein

Sunday

Monday

Tuesday

Wednesday – *write a list of things you are grateful for and why*

Thursday

Friday

Saturday

Week Reflection

What have I learnt this week?

What am I grateful for?

What emotions have I felt?

What distractions or fears have I encountered and how did I meet them?

Habit Tracker (out of 10)

Habit	M	T	W	T	F	S	S
Mood							
Purpose							
You Time							
Healthy Eating							
Drinking Water							
Exercise							

What have I rewarded myself with this week and what was it for?

How can I make next week even better and what do I need to prepare?

Week commencing – 26 September
This week -   I am showing gratitude for: 1.   2.   3.
I will make this week great by: 1.   2.   3.
This week's goals: 1.   2.   3.
Rewards if achieved: 1.   2.   3.
Positive affirmations: 1. *I am here in the present moment.*   2.   3.
Quote: *"Teachers open the door, but you must enter by yourself"* – Chinese Proverb

Sunday

Monday

Tuesday

Wednesday

Thursday – *do something physically active today*

Friday

Saturday

Week Reflection

What have I learnt this week?

What am I grateful for?

What emotions have I felt?

What distractions or fears have I encountered and how did I meet them?

Habit Tracker (out of 10)

Habit	M	T	W	T	F	S	S
Mood							
Purpose							
You Time							
Healthy Eating							
Drinking Water							
Exercise							

What have I rewarded myself with this week and what was it for?

How can I make next week even better and what do I need to prepare?

Week commencing – 3 October
This week -   I am showing gratitude for: 1.   2.   3.
I will make this week great by: 1.   2.   3.
This week's goals: 1.   2.   3.
Rewards if achieved: 1.   2.   3.
Positive affirmations: 1.   2.   3.
Quote: *"An investment in knowledge pays the best interest"* – Benjamin Franklin

Sunday

Monday

Tuesday

Wednesday

Thursday

Friday – *say something positive to everyone you meet today*

Saturday

Week Reflection

What have I learnt this week?

What am I grateful for?

What emotions have I felt?

What distractions or fears have I encountered and how did I meet them?

Habit Tracker (out of 10)

Habit	M	T	W	T	F	S	S
Mood							
Purpose							
You Time							
Healthy Eating							
Drinking Water							
Exercise							

What have I rewarded myself with this week and what was it for?

How can I make next week even better and what do I need to prepare?

Week commencing – 10 October
This week -   I am showing gratitude for: 1.   2.   3.
I will make this week great by: 1.   2.   3.
This week's goals: 1.   2.   3.
Rewards if achieved: 1.   2.   3.
Positive affirmations: 1.   2.   3.
Quote: *"The highest result of education is tolerance"* – Hellen Keller

Sunday
Monday
Tuesday
Wednesday
Thursday
Friday
Saturday – *take ten minutes to sit still and breathe*

Week Reflection

What have I learnt this week?

What am I grateful for?

What emotions have I felt?

What distractions or fears have I encountered and how did I meet them?

Habit Tracker (out of 10)

Habit	M	T	W	T	F	S	S
Mood							
Purpose							
You Time							
Healthy Eating							
Drinking Water							
Exercise							

What have I rewarded myself with this week and what was it for?

How can I make next week even better and what do I need to prepare?

Week commencing – 17 October
This week - I am showing gratitude for: 1. 2. 3.
I will make this week great by: 1. 2. 3.
This week's goals: 1. 2. 3.
Rewards if achieved: 1. 2. 3.
Positive affirmations: 1. 2. 3.
Quote: *"The beautiful thing about learning is that no one can take it away from you"* – B. B. King

Sunday – *look for the good in others and notice their strengths*

Monday

Tuesday

Wednesday

Thursday

Friday

Saturday

Week Reflection

What have I learnt this week?

What am I grateful for?

What emotions have I felt?

What distractions or fears have I encountered and how did I meet them?

Habit Tracker (out of 10)

Habit	M	T	W	T	F	S	S
Mood							
Purpose							
You Time							
Healthy Eating							
Drinking Water							
Exercise							

What have I rewarded myself with this week and what was it for?

How can I make next week even better and what do I need to prepare?

Week commencing – 24 October
This week -   I am showing gratitude for: 1.   2.   3.
I will make this week great by: 1.   2.   3.
This week's goals: 1.   2.   3.
Rewards if achieved: 1.   2.   3.
Positive affirmations: 1.   2.   3.
Quote: *"Education is simply the soul of a society as it passes from one generation to another"* – G.K. Chesterton

Sunday

Monday *Learn something new and share it with others*

Tuesday

Wednesday

Thursday

Friday

Saturday

Week Reflection

What have I learnt this week?

What am I grateful for?

What emotions have I felt?

What distractions or fears have I encountered and how did I meet them?

Habit Tracker (out of 10)

Habit	M	T	W	T	F	S	S
Mood							
Purpose							
You Time							
Healthy Eating							
Drinking Water							
Exercise							

What have I rewarded myself with this week and what was it for?

How can I make next week even better and what do I need to prepare?

Week commencing – 31 October

This week -
I am showing gratitude for:
1.
2.
3.

I will make this week great by:
1.
2.
3.

This week's goals:
1.
2.
3.

Rewards if achieved:
1.
2.
3.

Positive affirmations:
1.
2.
3.

Quote: *"The whole purpose of education is to turn mirrors into windows"* – Sydney J. Harris

Sunday

Monday

Tuesday *Thank three people you are grateful to and tell them why*

Wednesday

Thursday

Friday

Saturday

Week Reflection

What have I learnt this week?

What am I grateful for?

What emotions have I felt?

What distractions or fears have I encountered and how did I meet them?

Habit Tracker (out of 10)

Habit	M	T	W	T	F	S	S
Mood							
Purpose							
You Time							
Healthy Eating							
Drinking Water							
Exercise							

What have I rewarded myself with this week and what was it for?

How can I make next week even better and what do I need to prepare?

Week commencing – 7 November
This week - I am showing gratitude for: 1. 2. 3.
I will make this week great by: 1. 2. 3.
This week's goals: 1. 2. 3.
Rewards if achieved: 1. 2. 3.
Positive affirmations: 1. 2. 3.
Quote: *"The function of education is to teach one to think intensively and to think critically. Intelligence plus character – that is the goal of true education"* – Martin Luther King

Sunday

Monday

Tuesday

Wednesday *Get back in contact with an old friend*

Thursday

Friday

Saturday

Week Reflection

What have I learnt this week?

What am I grateful for?

What emotions have I felt?

What distractions or fears have I encountered and how did I meet them?

Habit Tracker (out of 10)

Habit	M	T	W	T	F	S	S
Mood							
Purpose							
You Time							
Healthy Eating							
Drinking Water							
Exercise							

What have I rewarded myself with this week and what was it for?

How can I make next week even better and what do I need to prepare?

Week commencing – 14 November
This week - I am showing gratitude for: 1. 2. 3.
I will make this week great by: 1. 2. 3.
This week's goals: 1. 2. 3.
Rewards if achieved: 1. 2. 3.
Positive affirmations: 1. 2. 3.
Quote: *"When you educate one person you can change a life, when you educate many you can change the world"*- Shai Reshef

Sunday

Monday

Tuesday

Wednesday

Thursday *Go to bed early to let yourself recharge*

Friday

Saturday

Week Reflection

What have I learnt this week?

What am I grateful for?

What emotions have I felt?

What distractions or fears have I encountered and how did I meet them?

Habit Tracker (out of 10)

Habit	M	T	W	T	F	S	S
Mood							
Purpose							
You Time							
Healthy Eating							
Drinking Water							
Exercise							

What have I rewarded myself with this week and what was it for?

How can I make next week even better and what do I need to prepare?

Week commencing – 21 November
This week -   I am showing gratitude for: 1.   2.   3.
I will make this week great by: 1.   2.   3.
This week's goals: 1.   2.   3.
Rewards if achieved: 1.   2.   3.
Positive affirmations: 1.   2.   3.
Quote: *"A man's mind, stretched by new ideas, may never return to its original dimensions."* - Oliver Wendell Holmes Jr.

Sunday
Monday
Tuesday
Wednesday
Thursday
Friday *Take a small step towards an important goal*
Saturday

Week Reflection

What have I learnt this week?

What am I grateful for?

What emotions have I felt?

What distractions or fears have I encountered and how did I meet them?

Habit Tracker (out of 10)

Habit	M	T	W	T	F	S	S
Mood							
Purpose							
You Time							
Healthy Eating							
Drinking Water							
Exercise							

What have I rewarded myself with this week and what was it for?

How can I make next week even better and what do I need to prepare?

Week commencing – 28 November
This week - I am showing gratitude for: 1. 2. 3.
I will make this week great by: 1. 2. 3.
This week's goals: 1. 2. 3.
Rewards if achieved: 1. 2. 3.
Positive affirmations: 1. 2. 3.
Quote: *"Anyone who has never made a mistake has never tried anything new."*- Albert Einstein

Sunday

Monday

Tuesday

Wednesday

Thursday

Friday

Saturday *Try something new out of your comfort zone*

Week Reflection

What have I learnt this week?

What am I grateful for?

What emotions have I felt?

What distractions or fears have I encountered and how did I meet them?

Habit Tracker (out of 10)

Habit	M	T	W	T	F	S	S
Mood							
Purpose							
You Time							
Healthy Eating							
Drinking Water							
Exercise							

What have I rewarded myself with this week and what was it for?

How can I make next week even better and what do I need to prepare?

Week commencing – 5 December
This week -   I am showing gratitude for: 1.   2.   3.
I will make this week great by: 1.   2.   3.
This week's goals: 1.   2.   3.
Rewards if achieved: 1.   2.   3.
Positive affirmations: 1.   2.   3.
Quote: *"He who opens a school door, closes a prison."* - Victor Hugo

Sunday *Do something fun and invite others to join you*
Monday
Tuesday
Wednesday
Thursday
Friday
Saturday

Week Reflection

What have I learnt this week?

What am I grateful for?

What emotions have I felt?

What distractions or fears have I encountered and how did I meet them?

Habit Tracker (out of 10)

Habit	M	T	W	T	F	S	S
Mood							
Purpose							
You Time							
Healthy Eating							
Drinking Water							
Exercise							

What have I rewarded myself with this week and what was it for?

How can I make next week even better and what do I need to prepare?

Week commencing – 12 December
This week - I am showing gratitude for: 1. 2. 3.
I will make this week great by: 1. 2. 3.
This week's goals: 1. 2. 3.
Rewards if achieved: 1. 2. 3.
Positive affirmations: 1. 2. 3.
Quote: *"Keep away from people who try to belittle your ambitions. Small people always do that, but the really great make you feel that you, too, can become great."*- Mark Twain

Sunday

Monday *Decide to lift people up rather than put them down*

Tuesday

Wednesday

Thursday

Friday

Saturday

Week Reflection

What have I learnt this week?

What am I grateful for?

What emotions have I felt?

What distractions or fears have I encountered and how did I meet them?

Habit Tracker (out of 10)

Habit	M	T	W	T	F	S	S
Mood							
Purpose							
You Time							
Healthy Eating							
Drinking Water							
Exercise							

What have I rewarded myself with this week and what was it for?

How can I make next week even better and what do I need to prepare?

Week commencing – 19 December

This week -
I am showing gratitude for:
1.
2.
3.

I will make this week great by:
1.
2.
3.

This week's goals:
1.
2.
3.

Rewards if achieved:
1.
2.
3.

Positive affirmations:
1. *I am doing a wonderful job*
2.
3.

Quote: *"Start where you are. Use what you have. Do what you can."* - Arthur Ashe

Sunday

Monday

Tuesday *Make something happen for a good cause*

Wednesday

Thursday

Friday –

Saturday

Week Reflection

What have I learnt this week?

What am I grateful for?

What emotions have I felt?

What distractions or fears have I encountered and how did I meet them?

Habit Tracker (out of 10)

Habit	M	T	W	T	F	S	S
Mood							
Purpose							
You Time							
Healthy Eating							
Drinking Water							
Exercise							

What have I rewarded myself with this week and what was it for?

How can I make next week even better and what do I need to prepare?

Week commencing – 26 December
This week - I am showing gratitude for: 1. 2. 3.
I will make this week great by: 1. 2. 3.
This week's goals: 1. 2. 3.
Rewards if achieved: 1. 2. 3.
Positive affirmations: 1. 2. 3.
Quote: *"Either you run the day or the day runs you."*- Jim Rohn

Sunday

Monday

Tuesday

Wednesday *Put away your devices and fully focus on those around you*

Thursday

Friday

Saturday

Week Reflection

What have I learnt this week?

What am I grateful for?

What emotions have I felt?

What distractions or fears have I encountered and how did I meet them?

Habit Tracker (out of 10)

Habit	M	T	W	T	F	S	S
Mood							
Purpose							
You Time							
Healthy Eating							
Drinking Water							
Exercise							

What have I rewarded myself with this week and what was it for?

How can I make next week even better and what do I need to prepare?

Week commencing – 2 January
This week -   I am showing gratitude for: 1.   2.   3.
I will make this week great by: 1.   2.   3.
This week's goals: 1.   2.   3.
Rewards if achieved: 1.   2.   3.
Positive affirmations: 1.   2.   3.
Quote: *"Education is the passport to the future, for tomorrow belongs to those who prepare for it today."*- Malcolm X

Sunday

Monday

Tuesday

Wednesday

Thursday *Say hello to a neighbour and get to know them better*

Friday

Saturday

Week Reflection

What have I learnt this week?

What am I grateful for?

What emotions have I felt?

What distractions or fears have I encountered and how did I meet them?

Habit Tracker (out of 10)

Habit	M	T	W	T	F	S	S
Mood							
Purpose							
You Time							
Healthy Eating							
Drinking Water							
Exercise							

What have I rewarded myself with this week and what was it for?

How can I make next week even better and what do I need to prepare?

Week commencing – 9 January
This week - I am showing gratitude for: 1. 2. 3.
I will make this week great by: 1. 2. 3.
This week's goals: 1. 2. 3.
Rewards if achieved: 1. 2. 3.
Positive affirmations: 1. 2. 3.
Quote: *"Your attitude, not your aptitude, will determine your altitude."*- Zig Ziglar

Sunday

Monday

Tuesday

Wednesday

Thursday

Friday *Challenge negative thoughts and look for the upside*

Saturday

Week Reflection

What have I learnt this week?

What am I grateful for?

What emotions have I felt?

What distractions or fears have I encountered and how did I meet them?

Habit Tracker (out of 10)

Habit	M	T	W	T	F	S	S
Mood							
Purpose							
You Time							
Healthy Eating							
Drinking Water							
Exercise							

What have I rewarded myself with this week and what was it for?

How can I make next week even better and what do I need to prepare?

Week commencing – 16 January
This week - I am showing gratitude for: 1. 2. 3.
I will make this week great by: 1. 2. 3.
This week's goals: 1. 2. 3.
Rewards if achieved: 1. 2. 3.
Positive affirmations: 1. 2. 3.
Quote: *"If you think education is expensive, try ignorance."* - Andy McIntyre

Sunday

Monday

Tuesday

Wednesday

Thursday

Friday

Saturday *How may people can you make smile today?*

Week Reflection

What have I learnt this week?

What am I grateful for?

What emotions have I felt?

What distractions or fears have I encountered and how did I meet them?

Habit Tracker (out of 10)

Habit	M	T	W	T	F	S	S
Mood							
Purpose							
You Time							
Healthy Eating							
Drinking Water							
Exercise							

What have I rewarded myself with this week and what was it for?

How can I make next week even better and what do I need to prepare?

Week commencing – 23 January
This week - I am showing gratitude for: 1. 2. 3.
I will make this week great by: 1. 2. 3.
This week's goals: 1. 2. 3.
Rewards if achieved: 1. 2. 3.
Positive affirmations: 1. 2. 3.
Quote: *"The only person who is educated is the one who has learned how to learn …and change."* - Carl Rogers

Sunday *Use a personal strength in a new way*

Monday

Tuesday

Wednesday

Thursday

Friday

Saturday

Week Reflection

What have I learnt this week?

What am I grateful for?

What emotions have I felt?

What distractions or fears have I encountered and how did I meet them?

Habit Tracker (out of 10)

Habit	M	T	W	T	F	S	S
Mood							
Purpose							
You Time							
Healthy Eating							
Drinking Water							
Exercise							

What have I rewarded myself with this week and what was it for?

How can I make next week even better and what do I need to prepare?

Week commencing – 30 January
This week - I am showing gratitude for: 1. 2. 3.
I will make this week great by: 1. 2. 3.
This week's goals: 1. 2. 3.
Rewards if achieved: 1. 2. 3.
Positive affirmations: 1. 2. 3.
Quote: *"The secret of getting started is breaking your complex overwhelming tasks into small manageable tasks, and then starting on the first one."*- Mark Twain

Sunday
Monday *Ask other people about things they have enjoyed recently*
Tuesday
Wednesday
Thursday
Friday
Saturday

Week Reflection

What have I learnt this week?

What am I grateful for?

What emotions have I felt?

What distractions or fears have I encountered and how did I meet them?

Habit Tracker (out of 10)

Habit	M	T	W	T	F	S	S
Mood							
Purpose							
You Time							
Healthy Eating							
Drinking Water							
Exercise							

What have I rewarded myself with this week and what was it for?

How can I make next week even better and what do I need to prepare?

Week commencing – 6 February

This week -
I am showing gratitude for:
1.
2.
3.

I will make this week great by:
1.
2.
3.

This week's goals:
1.
2.
3.

Rewards if achieved:
1.
2.
3.

Positive affirmations:
1.
2.
3.

Quote: "Education is a progressive discovery of our own ignorance." - Will Durant

Sunday

Monday

Tuesday *Write down your hopes and plans for the future*

Wednesday

Thursday

Friday

Saturday

Week Reflection

What have I learnt this week?

What am I grateful for?

What emotions have I felt?

What distractions or fears have I encountered and how did I meet them?

Habit Tracker (out of 10)

Habit	M	T	W	T	F	S	S
Mood							
Purpose							
You Time							
Healthy Eating							
Drinking Water							
Exercise							

What have I rewarded myself with this week and what was it for?

How can I make next week even better and what do I need to prepare?

Week commencing – 13 February

This week -
I am showing gratitude for:
1.
2.
3.

I will make this week great by:
1.
2.
3.

This week's goals:
1.
2.
3.

Rewards if achieved:
1.
2.
3.

Positive affirmations:
1.
2.
3.

Quote: *"Be miserable. Or motivate yourself. Whatever has to be done, it's always your choice."* - Wayne Dyer

Sunday

Monday

Tuesday

Wednesday *Set an intention to live with kindness and happiness*

Thursday

Friday

Saturday

Week Reflection

What have I learnt this week?

What am I grateful for?

What emotions have I felt?

What distractions or fears have I encountered and how did I meet them?

Habit Tracker (out of 10)

Habit	M	T	W	T	F	S	S
Mood							
Purpose							
You Time							
Healthy Eating							
Drinking Water							
Exercise							

What have I rewarded myself with this week and what was it for?

How can I make next week even better and what do I need to prepare?

Week commencing – 20 February
This week - I am showing gratitude for: 1. 2. 3.
I will make this week great by: 1. 2. 3.
This week's goals: 1. 2. 3.
Rewards if achieved: 1. 2. 3.
Positive affirmations: 1. 2. 3.
Quote: *"The difference between school and life? In school, you're taught a lesson and then given a test. In life, you're given a test that teaches you a lesson."*- Tom Bodett

Sunday
Monday
Tuesday
Wednesday
Thursday *Go outside and notice five things that are beautiful*
Friday
Saturday

Week Reflection

What have I learnt this week?

What am I grateful for?

What emotions have I felt?

What distractions or fears have I encountered and how did I meet them?

Habit Tracker (out of 10)

Habit	M	T	W	T	F	S	S
Mood							
Purpose							
You Time							
Healthy Eating							
Drinking Water							
Exercise							

What have I rewarded myself with this week and what was it for?

How can I make next week even better and what do I need to prepare?

Week commencing – 27 February
This week -   I am showing gratitude for: 1.   2.   3.
I will make this week great by: 1.   2.   3.
This week's goals: 1.   2.   3.
Rewards if achieved: 1.   2.   3.
Positive affirmations: 1.   2.   3.
Quote: *"We learn more by looking for the answer to a question and not finding it than we do from learning the answer itself."*- Lloyd Alexander

Sunday

Monday

Tuesday

Wednesday

Thursday

Friday *Cultivate a feeling of kindness towards others today*

Saturday

Week Reflection

What have I learnt this week?

What am I grateful for?

What emotions have I felt?

What distractions or fears have I encountered and how did I meet them?

Habit Tracker (out of 10)

Habit	M	T	W	T	F	S	S
Mood							
Purpose							
You Time							
Healthy Eating							
Drinking Water							
Exercise							

What have I rewarded myself with this week and what was it for?

How can I make next week even better and what do I need to prepare?

Week commencing – 6 March
This week - I am showing gratitude for: 1. 2. 3.
I will make this week great by: 1. 2. 3.
This week's goals: 1. 2. 3.
Rewards if achieved: 1. 2. 3.
Positive affirmations: 1. 2. 3.
Quote: *"Don't let what you cannot do interfere with what you can do."* - John R. Wooden

Sunday
Monday
Tuesday
Wednesday
Thursday
Friday
Saturday *Start today by appreciating you have a body and are alive*

Week Reflection

What have I learnt this week?

What am I grateful for?

What emotions have I felt?

What distractions or fears have I encountered and how did I meet them?

Habit Tracker (out of 10)

Habit	M	T	W	T	F	S	S
Mood							
Purpose							
You Time							
Healthy Eating							
Drinking Water							
Exercise							

What have I rewarded myself with this week and what was it for?

How can I make next week even better and what do I need to prepare?

Week commencing – 13 March
This week - I am showing gratitude for: 1. 2. 3.
I will make this week great by: 1. 2. 3.
This week's goals: 1. 2. 3.
Rewards if achieved: 1. 2. 3.
Positive affirmations: 1. 2. 3.
Quote: *"You will either step forward into growth, or you will step backward into safety."*- Abraham Maslow

Sunday *Take three calm breaths in every hour*

Monday

Tuesday

Wednesday

Thursday

Friday

Saturday

Week Reflection

What have I learnt this week?

What am I grateful for?

What emotions have I felt?

What distractions or fears have I encountered and how did I meet them?

Habit Tracker (out of 10)

Habit	M	T	W	T	F	S	S
Mood							
Purpose							
You Time							
Healthy Eating							
Drinking Water							
Exercise							

What have I rewarded myself with this week and what was it for?

How can I make next week even better and what do I need to prepare?

Week commencing – 20 March

This week -
I am showing gratitude for:
1.
2.
3.

I will make this week great by:
1.
2.
3.

This week's goals:
1.
2.
3.

Rewards if achieved:
1.
2.
3.

Positive affirmations:
1.
2.
3.

Quote: *"If a man empties his purse into his head, no man can take it away from him. An investment in knowledge always pays the best interest."* - Ben Franklin

Sunday
Monday Eat *mindfully today*
Tuesday
Wednesday
Thursday
Friday
Saturday

Week Reflection

What have I learnt this week?

What am I grateful for?

What emotions have I felt?

What distractions or fears have I encountered and how did I meet them?

Habit Tracker (out of 10)

Habit	M	T	W	T	F	S	S
Mood							
Purpose							
You Time							
Healthy Eating							
Drinking Water							
Exercise							

What have I rewarded myself with this week and what was it for?

How can I make next week even better and what do I need to prepare?

Week commencing – 27 March
This week -   I am showing gratitude for: 1.   2.   3.
I will make this week great by: 1.   2.   3.
This week's goals: 1.   2.   3.
Rewards if achieved: 1.   2.   3.
Positive affirmations: 1.   2.   3.
Quote: *"If people did not do silly things, nothing intelligent would ever get done."*- Ludwig Wittgenstein

Sunday

Monday

Tuesday *Listen to a piece of music without doing anything else*

Wednesday

Thursday

Friday

Saturday

Week Reflection

What have I learnt this week?

What am I grateful for?

What emotions have I felt?

What distractions or fears have I encountered and how did I meet them?

Habit Tracker (out of 10)

Habit	M	T	W	T	F	S	S
Mood							
Purpose							
You Time							
Healthy Eating							
Drinking Water							
Exercise							

What have I rewarded myself with this week and what was it for?

How can I make next week even better and what do I need to prepare?

Week commencing – 3 April
This week -   I am showing gratitude for: 1.   2.   3.
I will make this week great by: 1.   2.   3.
This week's goals: 1.   2.   3.
Rewards if achieved: 1.   2.   3.
Positive affirmations: 1.   2.   3.
Quote: *"Remember that failure is an event, not a person."* – Zig Ziglar

Sunday

Monday

Tuesday

Wednesday *Slow down and do something spontaneous*

Thursday

Friday

Saturday

Week Reflection

What have I learnt this week?

What am I grateful for?

What emotions have I felt?

What distractions or fears have I encountered and how did I meet them?

Habit Tracker (out of 10)

Habit	M	T	W	T	F	S	S
Mood							
Purpose							
You Time							
Healthy Eating							
Drinking Water							
Exercise							

What have I rewarded myself with this week and what was it for?

How can I make next week even better and what do I need to prepare?

Week commencing – 10 April
This week -   I am showing gratitude for: 1.   2.   3.
I will make this week great by: 1.   2.   3.
This week's goals: 1.   2.   3.
Rewards if achieved: 1.   2.   3.
Positive affirmations: 1.   2.   3.
Quote: *"If you don't design your own life plan, chances are you'll fall into someone else's plan. And guess what they have planned for you? Not much."* - Jim Rohn

Sunday

Monday

Tuesday

Wednesday

Thursday *When someone is speaking take in a big breath before you reply.*

Friday

Saturday

Week Reflection

What have I learnt this week?

What am I grateful for?

What emotions have I felt?

What distractions or fears have I encountered and how did I meet them?

Habit Tracker (out of 10)

Habit	M	T	W	T	F	S	S
Mood							
Purpose							
You Time							
Healthy Eating							
Drinking Water							
Exercise							

What have I rewarded myself with this week and what was it for?

How can I make next week even better and what do I need to prepare?

Week commencing – 17 April
This week -   I am showing gratitude for: 1.   2.   3.
I will make this week great by: 1.   2.   3.
This week's goals: 1.   2.   3.
Rewards if achieved: 1.   2.   3.
Positive affirmations: 1.   2.   3.
Quote: *"You can teach a student a lesson for a day; but if you can teach him to learn by creating curiosity, he will continue the learning process as long as he lives."* - Clay P. Bedford

Sunday

Monday

Tuesday

Wednesday

Thursday

Friday *Stay fully present while you drink your tea of coffee today*

Saturday

Week Reflection

What have I learnt this week?

What am I grateful for?

What emotions have I felt?

What distractions or fears have I encountered and how did I meet them?

Habit Tracker (out of 10)

Habit	M	T	W	T	F	S	S
Mood							
Purpose							
You Time							
Healthy Eating							
Drinking Water							
Exercise							

What have I rewarded myself with this week and what was it for?

How can I make next week even better and what do I need to prepare?

Week commencing – 24 April
This week - I am showing gratitude for: 1. 2. 3.
I will make this week great by: 1. 2. 3.
This week's goals: 1. 2. 3.
Rewards if achieved: 1. 2. 3.
Positive affirmations: 1. 2. 3.
Quote: "A teacher affects eternity; he can never tell where his influence stops." - Henry B Adams

Sunday
Monday
Tuesday
Wednesday
Thursday
Friday
Saturday *Notice how you speak to yourself. Try to use nice words.*

Week Reflection							
What have I learnt this week?							
What am I grateful for?							
What emotions have I felt?							
What distractions or fears have I encountered and how did I meet them?							

Habit Tracker (out of 10)

Habit	M	T	W	T	F	S	S
Mood							
Purpose							
You Time							
Healthy Eating							
Drinking Water							
Exercise							

What have I rewarded myself with this week and what was it for?

How can I make next week even better and what do I need to prepare?

Week commencing – 1 May
This week -
I am showing gratitude for:
1.
2.
3.
I will make this week great by:
1.
2.
3.
This week's goals:
1.
2.
3.
Rewards if achieved:
1.
2.
3.
Positive affirmations:
1.
2.
3.
Quote: *"To teach is to learn twice."* - Joseph Joubert

Sunday *Feel the cool breeze or warmth of the sun on your face.*	
Monday	
Tuesday	
Wednesday	
Thursday	
Friday	
Saturday	

Week Reflection							

What have I learnt this week?

What am I grateful for?

What emotions have I felt?

What distractions or fears have I encountered and how did I meet them?

Habit Tracker (out of 10)							
Habit	M	T	W	T	F	S	S
Mood							
Purpose							
You Time							
Healthy Eating							
Drinking Water							
Exercise							

What have I rewarded myself with this week and what was it for?

How can I make next week even better and what do I need to prepare?

Week commencing – 8 May
This week - I am showing gratitude for: 1. 2. 3.
I will make this week great by: 1. 2. 3.
This week's goals: 1. 2. 3.
Rewards if achieved: 1. 2. 3.
Positive affirmations: 1. 2. 3.
Quote: *"Do not confine your children to your own learning, for they were born in another time."* - Chinese proverb

Sunday

Monday *Stop. Breathe. Notice. Repeat*

Tuesday

Wednesday

Thursday

Friday

Saturday

Week Reflection

What have I learnt this week?

What am I grateful for?

What emotions have I felt?

What distractions or fears have I encountered and how did I meet them?

Habit Tracker (out of 10)

Habit	M	T	W	T	F	S	S
Mood							
Purpose							
You Time							
Healthy Eating							
Drinking Water							
Exercise							

What have I rewarded myself with this week and what was it for?

How can I make next week even better and what do I need to prepare?

Week commencing – 15 May
This week - I am showing gratitude for: 1. 2. 3.
I will make this week great by: 1. 2. 3.
This week's goals: 1. 2. 3.
Rewards if achieved: 1. 2. 3.
Positive affirmations: 1. 2. 3.
Quote: *"What we learn with pleasure we never forget."* - Alfred Mercier

Sunday

Monday

Tuesday *Enjoy doing tasks more mindfully today*

Wednesday

Thursday

Friday

Saturday

Week Reflection

What have I learnt this week?

What am I grateful for?

What emotions have I felt?

What distractions or fears have I encountered and how did I meet them?

Habit Tracker (out of 10)

Habit	M	T	W	T	F	S	S
Mood							
Purpose							
You Time							
Healthy Eating							
Drinking Water							
Exercise							

What have I rewarded myself with this week and what was it for?

How can I make next week even better and what do I need to prepare?

Week commencing – 22 May
This week - I am showing gratitude for: 1. 2. 3.
I will make this week great by: 1. 2. 3.
This week's goals: 1. 2. 3.
Rewards if achieved: 1. 2. 3.
Positive affirmations: 1. 2. 3.
Quote: *"Why should society feel responsible only for the education of children, and not for the education of all adults of every age?"*- Erich Fromm

Sunday

Monday

Tuesday

Wednesday *Stop and look at the clouds or sky for ten minutes.*

Thursday

Friday

Saturday

Week Reflection

What have I learnt this week?

What am I grateful for?

What emotions have I felt?

What distractions or fears have I encountered and how did I meet them?

Habit Tracker (out of 10)

Habit	M	T	W	T	F	S	S
Mood							
Purpose							
You Time							
Healthy Eating							
Drinking Water							
Exercise							

What have I rewarded myself with this week and what was it for?

How can I make next week even better and what do I need to prepare?

Week commencing – 29 May
This week -   I am showing gratitude for: 1.   2.   3.
I will make this week great by: 1.   2.   3.
This week's goals: 1.   2.   3.
Rewards if achieved: 1.   2.   3.
Positive affirmations: 1.   2.   3.
Quote: *"Children have never been very good at listening to their elders, but they have never failed to imitate them."* - James Baldwin

Sunday

Monday

Tuesday

Wednesday

Thursday *Do something creative that absorbs your attention*

Friday

Saturday

Week Reflection

What have I learnt this week?

What am I grateful for?

What emotions have I felt?

What distractions or fears have I encountered and how did I meet them?

Habit Tracker (out of 10)

Habit	M	T	W	T	F	S	S
Mood							
Purpose							
You Time							
Healthy Eating							
Drinking Water							
Exercise							

What have I rewarded myself with this week and what was it for?

How can I make next week even better and what do I need to prepare?

Week commencing – 5 June
This week -   I am showing gratitude for: 1.   2.   3.
I will make this week great by: 1.   2.   3.
This week's goals: 1.   2.   3.
Rewards if achieved: 1.   2.   3.
Positive affirmations: 1.   2.   3.
Quote: *"Example is not the main thing in influencing others. It is the only thing."*- Albert Schweitzer

| Sunday |
| Monday |
| Tuesday |
| Wednesday |
| Thursday |
| Friday *Spot three things you find unusual or pleasant* |
| Saturday |

Week Reflection

What have I learnt this week?

What am I grateful for?

What emotions have I felt?

What distractions or fears have I encountered and how did I meet them?

Habit Tracker (out of 10)

Habit	M	T	W	T	F	S	S
Mood							
Purpose							
You Time							
Healthy Eating							
Drinking Water							
Exercise							

What have I rewarded myself with this week and what was it for?

How can I make next week even better and what do I need to prepare?

Week commencing – 12 June
This week -   I am showing gratitude for: 1.   2.   3.
I will make this week great by: 1.   2.   3.
This week's goals: 1.   2.   3.
Rewards if achieved: 1.   2.   3.
Positive affirmations: 1.   2.   3.
Quote: *"Too often we give children answers to remember rather than problems to solve."* -Roger Lewin

| Sunday |
| Monday |
| Tuesday |
| Wednesday |
| Thursday |
| Friday |
| Saturday *If you find yourself rushing, try to slow down* |

Week Reflection

What have I learnt this week?

What am I grateful for?

What emotions have I felt?

What distractions or fears have I encountered and how did I meet them?

Habit Tracker (out of 10)

Habit	M	T	W	T	F	S	S
Mood							
Purpose							
You Time							
Healthy Eating							
Drinking Water							
Exercise							

What have I rewarded myself with this week and what was it for?

How can I make next week even better and what do I need to prepare?

Week commencing – 19 June
This week -   I am showing gratitude for: 1.   2.   3.
I will make this week great by: 1.   2.   3.
This week's goals: 1.   2.   3.
Rewards if achieved: 1.   2.   3.
Positive affirmations: 1.   2.   3.
Quote: *"The best teachers are those who show you where to look but don't tell you what to see."* - Alexandra K. Trenfor

Sunday *Listen carefully to someone to really hear what they want to say*	
Monday	
Tuesday	
Wednesday	
Thursday	
Friday	
Saturday	

Week Reflection

What have I learnt this week?

What am I grateful for?

What emotions have I felt?

What distractions or fears have I encountered and how did I meet them?

Habit Tracker (out of 10)

Habit	M	T	W	T	F	S	S
Mood							
Purpose							
You Time							
Healthy Eating							
Drinking Water							
Exercise							

What have I rewarded myself with this week and what was it for?

How can I make next week even better and what do I need to prepare?

Week commencing – 26 June
This week - I am showing gratitude for: 1. 2. 3.
I will make this week great by: 1. 2. 3.
This week's goals: 1. 2. 3.
Rewards if achieved: 1. 2. 3.
Positive affirmations: 1. 2. 3.
Quote: *"Children are apt to live up to what you believe of them."* - Lady Bird Johnson

Sunday
Monday *Appreciate the simple things in life*
Tuesday
Wednesday
Thursday
Friday
Saturday

Week Reflection

What have I learnt this week?

What am I grateful for?

What emotions have I felt?

What distractions or fears have I encountered and how did I meet them?

Habit Tracker (out of 10)

Habit	M	T	W	T	F	S	S
Mood							
Purpose							
You Time							
Healthy Eating							
Drinking Water							
Exercise							

What have I rewarded myself with this week and what was it for?

How can I make next week even better and what do I need to prepare?

Week commencing – 3 July
This week - I am showing gratitude for: 1. 2. 3.
I will make this week great by: 1. 2. 3.
This week's goals: 1. 2. 3.
Rewards if achieved: 1. 2. 3.
Positive affirmations: 1. 2. 3.
Quote: *"Nine tenths of education is encouragement."* - Anatole France

Sunday
Monday
Tuesday *Have a device free day and enjoy it with others*
Wednesday
Thursday
Friday
Saturday

Week Reflection
What have I learnt this week?
What am I grateful for?
What emotions have I felt?
What distractions or fears have I encountered and how did I meet them?

Habit Tracker (out of 10)

Habit	M	T	W	T	F	S	S
Mood							
Purpose							
You Time							
Healthy Eating							
Drinking Water							
Exercise							

What have I rewarded myself with this week and what was it for?

How can I make next week even better and what do I need to prepare?

Week commencing – 10 July
This week - I am showing gratitude for: 1. 2. 3.
I will make this week great by: 1. 2. 3.
This week's goals: 1. 2. 3.
Rewards if achieved: 1. 2. 3.
Positive affirmations: 1. 2. 3.
Quote: *"If someone is going down the wrong road, he doesn't need motivation to speed him up. What he needs is education to turn him around."* - Jim Rohn

Sunday

Monday

Tuesday

Wednesday *Take an unusual route and notice something different*

Thursday

Friday

Saturday

Week Reflection
What have I learnt this week?
What am I grateful for?
What emotions have I felt?
What distractions or fears have I encountered and how did I meet them?

Habit Tracker (out of 10)							
Habit	M	T	W	T	F	S	S
Mood							
Purpose							
You Time							
Healthy Eating							
Drinking Water							
Exercise							

What have I rewarded myself with this week and what was it for?

How can I make next week even better and what do I need to prepare?

Week commencing – 17 July
This week -   I am showing gratitude for: 1.   2.   3.
I will make this week great by: 1.   2.   3.
This week's goals: 1.   2.   3.
Rewards if achieved: 1.   2.   3.
Positive affirmations: 1.   2.   3.
Quote: *"Treat people as if they were what they ought to be, and you help them to become what they are capable of becoming."* - Goethe

Sunday

Monday

Tuesday

Wednesday

Thursday *Notice when you are tired and take a break*

Friday

Saturday

Week Reflection

What have I learnt this week?

What am I grateful for?

What emotions have I felt?

What distractions or fears have I encountered and how did I meet them?

Habit Tracker (out of 10)

Habit	M	T	W	T	F	S	S
Mood							
Purpose							
You Time							
Healthy Eating							
Drinking Water							
Exercise							

What have I rewarded myself with this week and what was it for?

How can I make next week even better and what do I need to prepare?

Week commencing – 24 July
This week -   I am showing gratitude for: 1.   2.   3.
I will make this week great by: 1.   2.   3.
This week's goals: 1.   2.   3.
Rewards if achieved: 1.   2.   3.
Positive affirmations: 1.   2.   3.
Quote: *"I believe that education is all about being excited about something. Seeing passion and enthusiasm helps push an educational message. "*- Steve Irwin

Sunday

Monday

Tuesday

Wednesday

Thursday

Friday *Make a list of the amazing things you take for granted*

Saturday

Week Reflection

What have I learnt this week?

What am I grateful for?

What emotions have I felt?

What distractions or fears have I encountered and how did I meet them?

Habit Tracker (out of 10)

Habit	M	T	W	T	F	S	S
Mood							
Purpose							
You Time							
Healthy Eating							
Drinking Water							
Exercise							

What have I rewarded myself with this week and what was it for?

How can I make next week even better and what do I need to prepare?

Week commencing – 31 July
This week -   I am showing gratitude for: 1.   2.   3.
I will make this week great by: 1.   2.   3.
This week's goals: 1.   2.   3.
Rewards if achieved: 1.   2.   3.
Positive affirmations: 1.   2.   3.
Quote: *"Any book that helps a child to form a habit of reading, to make reading one of his deep and continuing needs, is good for him."* - Maya Angelou

Sunday
Monday
Tuesday
Wednesday
Thursday
Friday
Saturday *Tune into your feelings without judging or trying to change*

Week Reflection							
What have I learnt this week?							
What am I grateful for?							
What emotions have I felt?							
What distractions or fears have I encountered and how did I meet them?							

Habit Tracker (out of 10)							
Habit	M	T	W	T	F	S	S
Mood							
Purpose							
You Time							
Healthy Eating							
Drinking Water							
Exercise							

What have I rewarded myself with this week and what was it for?

How can I make next week even better and what do I need to prepare?

Week commencing – 7 August
This week - I am showing gratitude for: 1. 2. 3.
I will make this week great by: 1. 2. 3.
This week's goals: 1. 2. 3.
Rewards if achieved: 1. 2. 3.
Positive affirmations: 1. 2. 3.
Quote: *"The key to everything is patience. You get the chicken by hatching the egg — not by smashing it."* - Arnold Glasow

Sunday *Bring to mind all the people you love and care about*
Monday
Tuesday
Wednesday
Thursday
Friday
Saturday

Week Reflection

What have I learnt this week?

What am I grateful for?

What emotions have I felt?

What distractions or fears have I encountered and how did I meet them?

Habit Tracker (out of 10)

Habit	M	T	W	T	F	S	S
Mood							
Purpose							
You Time							
Healthy Eating							
Drinking Water							
Exercise							

What have I rewarded myself with this week and what was it for?

How can I make next week even better and what do I need to prepare?

Week commencing – 14 August

This week -

I am showing gratitude for:
1.
2.
3.

I will make this week great by:
1.
2.
3.

This week's goals:
1.
2.
3.

Rewards if achieved:
1.
2.
3.

Positive affirmations:
1.
2.
3.

Quote: *"It is impossible for a man to learn what he thinks he already knows."* - Epictetus

Sunday

Monday *Appreciate your hands and all the things they enable you to do*

Tuesday

Wednesday

Thursday

Friday

Saturday

Week Reflection

What have I learnt this week?

What am I grateful for?

What emotions have I felt?

What distractions or fears have I encountered and how did I meet them?

Habit Tracker (out of 10)

Habit	M	T	W	T	F	S	S
Mood							
Purpose							
You Time							
Healthy Eating							
Drinking Water							
Exercise							

What have I rewarded myself with this week and what was it for?

How can I make next week even better and what do I need to prepare?

Week commencing – 21 August
This week - I am showing gratitude for: 1. 2. 3.
I will make this week great by: 1. 2. 3.
This week's goals: 1. 2. 3.
Rewards if achieved: 1. 2. 3.
Positive affirmations: 1. 2. 3.
Quote: *"If the only tool you have is a hammer, you tend to see every problem as a nail."* - Abraham Maslow

Sunday	
Monday	
Tuesday *Scan down your body and notice what it is feeling*	
Wednesday	
Thursday	
Friday	
Saturday	

Week Reflection

What have I learnt this week?

What am I grateful for?

What emotions have I felt?

What distractions or fears have I encountered and how did I meet them?

Habit Tracker (out of 10)

Habit	M	T	W	T	F	S	S
Mood							
Purpose							
You Time							
Healthy Eating							
Drinking Water							
Exercise							

What have I rewarded myself with this week and what was it for?

How can I make next week even better and what do I need to prepare?

Well done you have made it, not only through the school year but also the summer holidays, hopefully you are refreshed and ready for a new school year.

Like this journal? Scan the QR code below for other journals available.

www.chrisallton.co.uk/journals

Printed in Great Britain
by Amazon